THIS JOURNAL BELONGS TO:

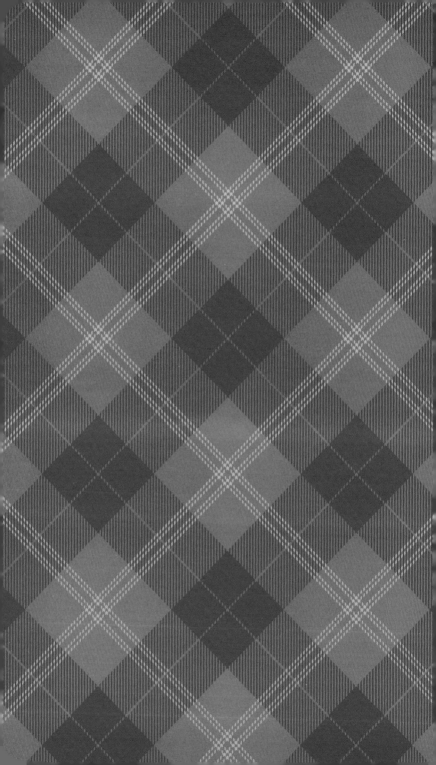

A DOG
WAGS
ITS TAIL
WITH ITS
HEART.

MARTIN BUXBAUM

NO MATTER

HOW LITTLE MONEY AND HOW
FEW POSSESSIONS YOU OWN,

HAVING A DOG
MAKES YOU RICH.

⊶ LOUIS SABIN

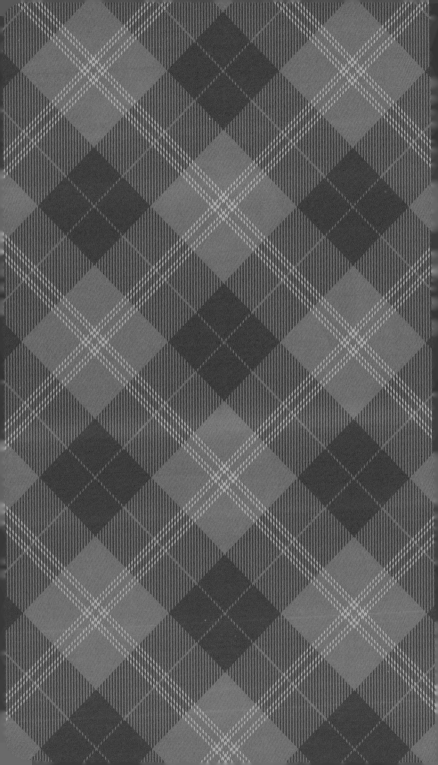

I THINK DOGS ARE THE MOST

AMAZING CREATURES...

THEY ARE THE

ROLE MODEL

FOR BEING ALIVE.

GILDA RADNER

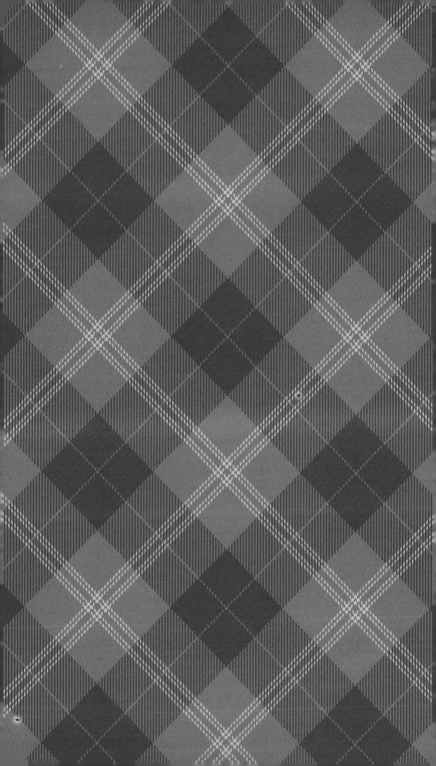

IN A PERFECT WORLD,
EVERY DOG
WOULD HAVE A HOME AND
EVERY HOME
WOULD HAVE A DOG.

— UNKNOWN

A DOG IS THE
ONLY THING ON EARTH
THAT LOVES YOU
MORE THAN
HE LOVES HIMSELF.

JOSH BILLINGS

IF THERE ARE NO
DOGS IN HEAVEN,
THEN WHEN I DIE I WANT
TO GO WHERE THEY WENT.

— WILL ROGERS

DOGS ARE NOT
OUR WHOLE LIFE,
BUT THEY MAKE
OUR LIVES WHOLE.

ROGER CARAS